Why are the Dandelions Weeds?

Kathleen O'Connell Chesto

D1316891

Liguori

ONE LIGUORI DRIVE
LIGUORI MO 63057-9999
314.464.2500

ISBN 0-7648-0406-5
Library of Congress Catalog Card Number: 98-75393

Cover design by Ross M. Sherman
Interior illustrations by Brian Calvey

to my Mom and Dad

Acknowledgments

This book could not have been written without the cooperation of Twenty-Third Publications who allowed me to use material that has previously appeared in the following videos: *Family Spirituality*; *Advent: A Time to Hope*; *Lent: A Time to Forgive*; and *Easter Season: A Time to Remember*. I am also grateful to *The Catechist's Connection* for permission to use stories from articles written for them.

I wish to thank Robert Heyer of Sheed & Ward for his help in making this book a reality, for assisting in creating its format, and for his many "ing" words.

I also want to thank the families who have touched my life and affirmed my own sense of family, especially Jonathan, Rebecca and Elizabeth, without whom there would be no stories, and, most importantly, Ed, without whom there would be no Jon, Becky or Liz.

Contents

Part III: Belonging

Part IV: Journeying

Part V: Becoming

Introduction

I removed the thermometer from Becky's mouth as she lay curled up miserably on the couch. 104 degrees.

"I feel so awful, Mom," she whispered hoarsely.

"Fevers are good for you," her unsympathetic older brother chimed in. "We need fevers. Without fevers, the human race couldn't survive."

"That may be true, Jon," I responded, "but they can be pretty miserable while you are living with them."

A slow grin crossed his face. "Sort of like kids, huh, Mom?"

This is a collection of stories from those years of "living with them." They have become kernels for articles, structures for videos, highlights for lectures. After many years of study and two theology degrees, I am convinced that most of what I know about God and most of what I believe about the sacredness of living, I have learned from my children.

The power of any story lies in its ability to put us in touch with our own stories. A tale tugs at our hearts because we catch a glimpse of ourselves, or some universal truth, hidden within the particulars of someone else's story. If these stories ring true, it will be because you recognize within them your own experience. You have heard them before; you have lived them with your own children.

These are family stories, reflections on important moments in family living, not necessarily the moments the rest of the world would choose as significant: new siblings, first bikes, tooth fairies, braces, and college. Several of them are challenges and insights offered to us by our children, insights they themselves did not understand and probably won't understand until they have a child of their own to teach them. Some are simply the innocent, startling things that children say, comments that can become moments of prayer and windows to the sacred, if we let them.

There was a time in my life when I firmly believed that God had given me children so that I might raise them as Christian, and it was an awesome, holy task. Those of us called to it had a profound work to accomplish. I still think parenting is awesome, but my confrontation with my son over the dandelions has given me a far different, far humbler view of my own role in this process. God didn't give me children to raise them as Christian; God gave me children to raise me as Christian! God knew I wasn't going to make it without them.

You have probably already discovered that same truth for yourself. Your children have shared sacred moments with you that have touched the very core of your being. These are the moments I have tried to capture in these stories, moments of insight, moments of reflection, moments of challenge.

Grouping the stories proved difficult. Chronologically, a family with differently aged children can be in several different stages simultaneously (at least, we always seem to be), and this was never intended to be a book about stages of development. Theoretically, there may be several strands of theological and psychological themes here, but this is a story book, not a text book. It is not an explanation of my well-thought out conclusions, based on the stories in our lives; it is the stories themselves, waiting for your own insights and conclusions, and your own stories.

In the end, I chose to group the stories under five themes common to family life, with a brief explanation of the connecting idea at the beginning of each section. My choice was arbitrary; I did it because it fit the stories, not because I saw these themes as five essentials for healthy family living. Some of the stories could easily have fit into several sections, some did not really fit anywhere at all. This, in itself, is a reflection of family life; families are messy.

I believe God talks to each of us through the mouths of our children and through the ordinary events that fill our lives as family. This collection of stories is a simple invitation to listen.

Note: Because these stories date back in time to the early 70's, some of the God language is sexist. In many cases, it was impossible to change the language without doing violence to the stories or to the people we were at that moment in time.

Part I

Wondering

Wondering

To see a world in a grain of sand
And heaven in a wild flower,
To hold infinity in the palm of your hand
And eternity in an hour.
    —William Blake, *Songs of Innocence*

Young children have a unique vision of reality. They have not heard all the worn out answers we traditionally give to life, all the tattered explanations that are supposed to satisfy, and so they are free to ask their own questions. It is this "Why" that frequently makes us stop and reconsider much of what we have always taken for granted; it is this "Why" that encourages us to grow.

A child's vision of the world is marked by a sense of wonder, a wonder that most of us lost long before we knew what it was we had. Life is celebrated and cherished wherever it is found. I know a two-year-old who wants to be a tree when he grows up, and who practises standing very still and tall on his lawn. I remember watching my own son at two, conversing for the better part of an hour with a spider that was weaving a web in the corner of his room. Only when he was quite sure the spider understood, would he consent to move it to a spot outside the house.

The stories in this section offer a child's view of reality. Our children invite us to look again with wonder on an old world that is made new through their eyes, to ask more searching questions, and to never, never accept that the dandelions are weeds simply because some adult said so.

Why Are the Dandelions Weeds?

It was the "era of the lawn" in our marriage, that time when you own your first new home and nothing is quite as important as the lawn. For one summer you cut and weed, and fertilize and water, so that you can cut and weed some more. At the end of that time, if you are at all like us, you decide that crabgrass is green and will do just fine.

We were still weeding. Ed was outside digging up the dandelion roots, putting powder from a green box into the holes. (The box promised the dandelions would not grow back, but no one had told the dandelions!) I was in the house with the baby when three-year-old Jon appeared at the back door, hands filled with wilted blossoms, tears streaming down his face.

"Mommy! Daddy is digging up all the flowers."

"Those aren't flowers," my answer came too quickly. "Those are weeds."

"Why?"

Why are the dandelions weeds? Since I had no idea, I did what every good mother would do in that situation. I hugged him and told him to go outside and play and I would think about it.

I did think about it. Why were the dandelions weeds? To my three-year-old, they must have looked just like the marigolds we were planting all along the walk. Why had I given my son such a confusing idea?

Soon, I felt, rather than saw him beside me. (They have a tendency to grow out of your side at three.) I looked down and found huge, accusing brown eyes looking up at me, as my son said fiercely, "I know why the dandelions are weeds."

Since I still didn't know why, I asked him.

"Why, Jonathan?"

"It's because they don't grow where you want them to!"

Which is precisely why the dandelions are weeds!

*　　　*　　　*

How easy it is, God, to label our children "weeds" when they don't grow the way we wanted them to!

Being Home When God Comes

It was one of the few peaceful moments we had had together, my two and a half year old son and I, since the new baby sister had come into his life. We finished up the lunch dishes quietly as I struggled for the words to let him know how important, how special, he still was in our lives. How do you reassure a misty-eyed toddler that he has not lost his unique place in the universe?

"Jonathan, did you know that before you were born, Mommy and Daddy had no baby at all and we wanted one so badly. We didn't care then if it was a girl or a boy, if he had curly hair or straight hair, blue eyes or brown eyes. We just wanted a baby. But now that you are here," I paused to give him a hug, "we are so glad God sent us you."

He looked up at me, eyes sparkling with love as he said,

"And I'm so glad, Mommy, that you stayed home the day God came."

*   *   *

How many of your gifts, God, have I missed completely because I was not "home" when you came? Help me to be as present as my son believes I am.

Forgiveness

Five-year-old Becky came into the kitchen with a question.

"Mommy, is God a grown-up or a parent?"

Confused, I asked her if there was a difference between being a grown-up or a parent.

"Oh, yes," she replied. "Grown-ups love you when you're good. Parents love you anyway."

*   *   *

God, could you ever be less for your children than I would choose to be for mine?

My People

My mother answered the phone and heard a tragic little voice on the other end say:

"Grandma, I've lost my people."

My people, my people, what have I done to you,
And in what have I offended you?

"Jon, I didn't know you had people."

"Oh, yes, Grandma, and it doesn't work without them."

They were Fisher-Price "people" to ride in the cars and operate his little garage. He had left them at his grandparents on our visit, and no prophet ever wept more bitterly over the loss of a people. They were quickly discovered and carefully shipped.

*   *   *

Not all people will be returned to you so easily, my Son, but it is well that you learned young that nothing works very well without them.

9

Heaven . . .

The death of our young neighbor left three year old Jon devastated.

"But where is Rose, Mommy?"

"Rose is in heaven."

"But where is heaven?"

"Heaven is where God is."

It was a copout answer, but how could I explain to my little one what I didn't understand myself?

"Is she happy, Mommy?"

"Oh yes, very happy. Everyone is happy in heaven"

"But where is Bob?" Bob was Rose's husband.

"Bob is in New Haven." I should have recognized the trap before I walked into it.

"But how can Rose be happy in heaven if Bob is in New Haven?"

How long does it take to learn to accept all the old cliches, to learn not to ask the unspeakable questions?

As I tucked him into bed that night, there was a strange peace in his smile.

"I figured out where heaven is, Mommy."

"Oh?"

"You said that heaven is where God is, right? Well then, heaven is in my heart. And those we love, if we remember them . . ."

He left the question unfinished, "Do they live forever in our hearts?"

*　　　*　　　*

Years later, Becky brought home a startlingly similar conclusion on an exam paper. She had been reading *The American Dream* by Edward Albee, a strange play in which an unloving couple is deciding to put their mother away in a home simply to get rid of her. As the old woman leaves, she takes everything with her, including the hallway, her room, and anything that had been touched by her presence. The test asked why she chose to do this.

Becky was sure she knew why.

"I think she had to, Mom. She couldn't leave any part of her behind because there was no one left who would cherish the memories."

*　　　*　　　*

I believe in the resurrection of the dead and in life everlasting. But I suspect that whether or not we live on in this world depends on whether or not there are those who "cherish the memories."

"We remember, Lord, those who have died . . ." has taken on a whole new meaning in my life.

Too Young for Communion

I started taking Liz to daily Mass when she was only two. There was something about the intimacy of the environment that made the exclusion from Communion far more painful for her than it was on Sundays. She would put her small hand over my mouth and cry softly as we returned from the altar.

At the kiss of peace one morning, she dodged out of the pew and into the sanctuary, holding her arms up to our pastor, as he approached the community. He bent down and embraced her lovingly. There were no tears at Communion that morning, or any day after, as her kiss of peace became a ritual. It was as if you could hear her thinking:

The mystery is great
And I
Too small to understand
They say.
And so, you hold him in your hand,
My Lord!
And turn me away.
But Jesus is great
And I
Small enough to see a truth
The grownups sometimes miss
And so
I run to greet My Lord,
And receive him
In your kiss.

Eucharistic People

I walked into the bedroom and found two-year-old Liz celebrating Mass. A red plaid scarf hung around her neck and on a table in front of her she had a small brass candlestick that could have resembled a chalice. She was holding a little plastic plate above the candlestick and saying over and over again: "This is my body."

Unwilling to interrupt anything so important, I waited until she had finished and then asked softly, "Did you want to change that plate into Jesus?"

"Oh, no, Mommy. I change Wizbef into Jesus. I change all the peoples into Jesus."

I was about to correct her when I realized she was right. What did it matter what happened to the bread and the wine if the people who celebrated with the bread and the wine were not changed into Jesus? Six graduate credits in sacramental theology and I had failed to understand what my child knew at two!

*   *   *

"I praise you Lord of heaven and earth for hiding these things from the learned and clever and choosing to reveal them to the little ones."
                                        —Luke 10:21

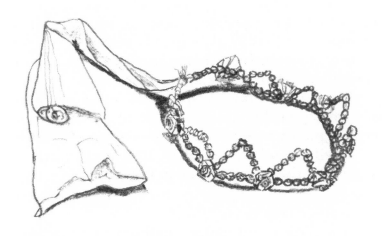

Magnificent

Ed's affectionate nickname for Liz as a baby was "Chubbo the Magnificent." While she was not a particularly chubby baby, the round face she inherited from her mother definitely gave that impression. The name was only used in love and carried none of the negative connotations "chubby" would hold for her at a later age.

On this particular morning, Liz and I were seated in the front pew at daily Mass. I was half listening to the homily as Father struggled to throw some light on a passage about the rebuilding of the temple. Liz had stopped paying attention, and the rest of the congregation was ready to join her, when Father described the temple as "magnificent." Recognizing an important word, she stood up on the bench, turned and faced the small community at Mass, and announced in the shrill voice with which two-year-old's tend to shatter silent moments, "My Daddy calls me magnificent."

The inattentive community was suddenly drawn together in a relaxed smile. Father gave up on his homily, walked over to Liz, and placing his hand gently on her head, said softly to the rest of the congregation, "Isn't that what being a Christian is all about? Each of us can say we have a Daddy who thinks we are magnificent."

*   *   *

"You are precious in my eyes, you are honored and I love you."   —Isaiah 43:4 JB

Rudolph

During Advent, we always made a Jesse tree as a family. Each night, we would tell the story of one character, make a symbol, and carry it to the living room in procession, with each child holding an Advent candle. Every night, a different child would get to choose the "Jesus song" we sang when we got to the tree. ("Jesus song" was our term for hymn.)

This particular night it was Becky's turn, and she said, "I choose Rudolph."

"Rudolph isn't a Jesus song, Becky," I objected.

"Yes it is, Mommy."

"No, Honey. You just think it is a Jesus song because we sing it at Christmas"

"It is, Mommy," she insisted with the stubbornness of five, and tears began to form in her eyes.

Ed, the more practical of the two of us, poked me in the ribs and said, "Who cares? This is supposed to be a happy family time and you are making the kid cry. Sing Rudolph. Anything can be a prayer."

So we sang Rudolph. Have you ever listened, I mean really listened, to the words of Rudolph, how he was an outcast and laughed at? It sounds a lot like the Suffering Servant Songs from Isaiah. And how did he come? As a light, on Christmas Eve, bringing us all good gifts.

As we finished, I said "Becky, I understand what you meant. You meant that Rudolph is like Jesus because he comes as a light on Christmas Eve and brings us all good gifts."

"Yes, Mommy." She sighed in relief that I finally understood. We had been listening to the same song, but Becky was the only one who heard. Rudolph has never been the same!

*   *   *

"Rudolph, with your nose so bright,
Won't you guide my sleigh tonight?"

Presents

Elizabeth wandered into the bedroom as I was wrapping Christmas presents. She had just celebrated her second birthday, so she knew all about the goodness of presents.

"Oooo! Presents! Wizbef's present?" she asked, touching a box that was already wrapped.

"No, that's Grandad's present."

"Grandad's birfday?"

"No. It's Jesus' birthday."

A puzzled frown creased her little forehead. She approached another box.

"Wizbef's present?"

"No, that's Jon's present."

"Jon's birfday?"

"No, it's Jesus' birthday."

The litany continued as she went around the room asking about each wrapped box, whose present was it, whose birthday was it. I answered distractedly, unaware of the dilemma I was creating for her.

Finally, she looked around at all the gifts and began reciting: "Jon's present, Jesus' birfday. Grandad's present, Jesus' birfday. Daddy's present, Jesus' birfday. Wizbef's present, Jesus' birfday."

As she paused in her reciting, I stopped what I was doing and looked up at her. She was obviously trying very hard to figure it all out. Suddenly a smile brightened her face.

"I Jesus, Jon Jesus, Grandad Jesus, Becky Jesus."

I was horrified and about to explain that wasn't true at all when I caught myself and thought, why else would we give one another presents on Jesus' birthday if not to say "Happy Birthday" to the Jesus in you, "Happy Birthday" to the Jesus in me? Christmas shopping will never be the same!

*   *   *

"Grown-ups never understand anything for themselves and it is tiresome for children to be always and forever explaining things to them."
—Antoine Saint-Exupery, *The Little Prince*

"You Listen Funny"

Jason stuttered—badly enough to make him a pariah, where the other kindergarteners were concerned. If Jon invited him to his birthday party, his other friends had threatened not to come. But Jason was also his friend. I wanted to remind him of that fact, to insist that he do what was right, but I did not have to return to kindergarten on Monday; I did not have to face the threat of no one coming to my party.

In the end, I kept quiet and Jason came, along with seven other noisy six-year-old boys. As the day drew to a close, they raced around the back yard in what appeared to be a deliberate attempt to insure that at least one of them would throw up the quantities of cake and ice cream they had consumed. I watched from the kitchen window as one of the bigger boys cornered the rather puny little Jason and started taunting, "You talk funny. You talk funny." A few others joined in the chant as I ran for the door. But my son was faster.

Facing up to the bully, he declared loudly, "He does not talk funny! You listen funny!"

meone tagged the assailant yelling "You're it!" and the game continued as if the incident had never happened. Perhaps disability, like beauty, is in the eye of the beholder. No one could deny that Jason stuttered; but whether or not he "talked funny," at least according to my son, depended on how you listened.

*   *   *

"It is only with the heart that one sees rightly."
—Antoine Saint-Expurey, *The Little Prince*

Handicapped Facilities

When I returned home in a wheel chair after my first major bout with multiple sclerosis, I was deeply concerned about my children's adjustment. I wondered how they felt about a mother who could only walk with two canes; I worried about their reactions to the physical adaptations necessary in the house. It was, after all, their home in which we were installing bars, ramps, and various equipment. Would they still be willing to share it with their friends?

The downstairs bathroom needed bars to help me off the toilet, bars for assistance in the shower, and a shower chair. The children made no comment as their Dad hammered and drilled, offering no hint of their feelings about the very visible alterations.

Shortly after the carpentry was finished, Liz invited another nine-year-old to visit. As soon as they had said hello, Liz rushed her friend down the hall, opened the bathroom door with a flourish, and announced proudly, "This is our handicapped bathroom. The regular one is upstairs."

*   *   *

*"Two men looked out through prison bars
One saw mud, the other saw stars."*
—Matt Talbot, *Viewpoint*

New York Drivers

Liz got into the car, frustrated and angry with the class she had just left.

"That guy teaches the way people in New York City drive!"

Confused, I asked her, "Exactly what does that comment mean?"

"He thinks you can teach by yelling. New Yorkers believe you can drive your car by honking the horn."

*   *   *

I suspect, Lord, there is a message in that for all of us, certified and non-certified teachers alike. Thinking we can teach by yelling is a lot like believing we can drive by honking the horn.

Who Do You Say That I Am?

As we walked out of church that morning, my fourteen-year-old said, "Well, who do you say he is?"

I had no idea what she was talking about. I guess my face mirrored the blankness of my mind, for she said; "You know, Mom, the gospel today about 'Who do you say I am'."

I had forgotten the gospel already, I am ashamed to say, but Liz had remembered and wanted to talk.

"That homily was so boring, Mom, I just made up my own while he was talking. You know what I think?"

"What?"

"I think Jesus is the caddy in the golf game of life."

"You want to explain that one a little, Liz?"

"Well, you don't need a caddy to play golf. He just sort of makes the game easier. Jesus is like that. Lots of good people live their lives never knowing him."

"Different people use their caddy in different ways. Some just let him carry the clubs when they get too heavy; some let him carry the burdens all the time, but never really talk to him. The smart ones are the ones who know they only get to play this course once and the caddy has been over it thousands of times. They ask for advice and help. I think Jesus is the caddy in the golf game of life."

*　　*　　*

If we took time to listen to the gospel according to our children, revelation might make a lot more sense in our lives.

Rainbows

"Mommy, Mommy! Come quick!"

My four-year-old practically dragged me out of the house to the front of the garage. A small puddle remained from the rain the night before. In the puddle was a film of oil.

"Look at the rainbow that fell out of the sky!" an awestruck little voice whispered to me.

*   *   *

Lord, when did I stop seeing the rainbows and start seeing only the oil?

Part II

Listening

Listening

Earth's crammed with heaven
And every common bush afire with God;
But only those who see take off their shoes.
The rest sit round it and pluck black-
   berries.
   —Elizabeth Barrett Browning, *Aurora Leigh*

Wonder is the beginning of prayer. I suspect
that children come to us as mystics; all the world
is a burning revelation and they stand in awe before it, their wonder a prayer of praise. Unwit-
tingly, we foster their spirituality. Every time we
pick up a crying baby, we teach the first, the most
important lesson on prayer: when you cry out,
someone answers. We teach them to play peek-a-
boo, and they learn to trust in a presence that they
can't always see. We teach clapping and waving,
and so they learn rituals to express their feelings.
It isn't until we attempt to teach prayer formally
that we lose sight of the reality, the burning
bushes and holy ground in our own back yards.

Prayer is primarily a relationship. It is at
least as much about the ability to listen and recognize the presence of God in our lives as it is about
asking God to change them. The following stories
are about the presence of prayer in our lives as
family, the sometimes humorous attempts to teach
it, and the God who always answers, almost in
spite of us.

Three Little Fish

It all started with:

"Down in the meadow in an iddy biddy pool
Lived three little fishies and a Mama fishy
too"

My Mom was giving Jon his bath and singing to him.

"Do you have three little fishies and a Mama fishy, Jon?" she asked.

"No, Grandma," he had answered solemnly.

"Well, you watch the mail. After I get home," she promised, "not right away, but in about a week, the postman will bring you a box with three little fishies and a Mama fishy too."

My mother went home that weekend. Jon began to check the mail box faithfully while my Mom proceeded to tear the state of Rhode Island apart looking for plastic fish for the tub. There were rubber duckies and plastic astronauts and dinosaurs, but no plastic fish. One store owner was very sympathetic; he thought it a shame that no one played with plastic fish any more, but he was certain there were none to be found. My Mom called a plastics factory to see what it would cost to have a mold made; she had promised and she hated to disappoint her grandson.

She was leaving a local discount store after talking to the manager for the third time, when she realized she had never prayed. Stopping in her tracks, she murmured gently, "Lord, I need three little fishies and a Mama fishy, too, for my grandson." As she stood there praying, the manager came running out of his office.

"Lady, I am so glad I caught you. We got this big closeout from a plastic factory. The stuff is in the infant department. I don't know what is there, but you might find something."

My Mom went to the back of the store and found three huge troughs stretching down the center of the aisles each containing thousands of carded plastic toys. It would take a year to go through them! Kneeling beside a container, she prayed quietly, "Lord, I need three little fishies and a Mama fishy too." Then she reached to the bottom and pulled out a card.

Under the plastic bubble on the card were three small plastic fish and one large one. Across the top, in dark print, it read, "Three little fishies and a Mama fishy too."

*   *   *

There are times when I have trouble belie
in the God who parted the Red Sea, provided
manna in the desert and water from the rock. But
I never have trouble believing in the God who could
provide three little fishies and a Mama fishy, too,
for a two-year-old boy.

Magic Prayers

Placing the plate of food before my one-year-old, I cautioned, "It's hot. Wait until after we pray." It was a familiar phrase. I said it every night, putting his food out first to cool while I finished setting the table. And tonight, like every other night, he waited until I was seated and we all joined hands around the table and prayed.

Two mouthfuls into his food, he spit out the spinach on his plate and yelled, "Hot Burn!" Then, reaching for our hands, he cried, "Pray! Pray!" Ed and I dissolved into laughter as we realized we had inadvertently taught our son that grace before meals cooled the food off!

*   *   *

Lord, how many of my prayers are for the same kind of "magic"? Teach me to pray, not to change my reality, but to be better able to live within it.

Mary Prayer

"Say the other Mary prayer, Mommy."

Two-year-old Jon was "saying" his prayers. Since he was very verbal, he had memorized the Lord's prayer and the Hail Mary easily and we said them every night. But there was no other Mary Prayer. Even though I was slightly paranoid about having him "learn" prayers, we had yet to reach the Memorare.

"What other Mary prayer, Jon? Say it for me."

"You know, the one that goes "Mary had a little lamb whose fleece . . ."

Prayers are not for reciting; they are for praying. While I was all for talking to God and listening quietly after we got done reciting, I had never made it clear that it all was prayer, not just the words we memorized and recited, or that all words we memorized and recited were not necessarily prayer.

A few weeks later, this same little one informed me he would not have time to "say prayers" that night. He had far too much to talk to God about! It was definitely time to rethink what I was teaching about prayer!

Dinner Guest

Summer bible school was over for the morning, and three-year-old Jon's teacher approached me with a slightly worried frown.

"I am not sure what I was doing wrong, Kathy. Jon usually loves class and has fun, but this morning . . . We were doing the story of Zacchaeus. I asked the children how they would feel if Jesus were coming to their house for supper. We made placemats for Jesus, just in case he ever came to our homes. Jon just sat there looking puzzled."

By now, Jon was at my side tugging on my skirt and saying, "Tell her, Mommy. Tell her."

Exasperated, I turned away from his teacher and looked down at him.

"Tell her what, Jon?"

"Tell her—Jesus eats supper at our house every night."

*   *   *

I had been the one who said the prayer every night, "Help us to remember, Lord, you are always the unseen guest at our table." It was my son who remembered and believed.

Reverence

As we approached the church on Sunday morning, I gave my usual word of caution to my super-active, super-noisy three-year-old: "Quiet down, now, we are going in God's house."

It was usually enough to quell the noise, at least momentarily. This particular morning, she looked at me with a puzzled frown.

"What's the matter," she responded, "Is He sick?"

I thought that you taught children reverence. I thought it was one of those things that was inculcated at an early age and explained carefully as time went on. I am not sure what I taught, but it wasn't reverence.

I was committed to being more careful with the baby. She would never hear those fateful words that had so confused her older sister! Liz would always be told that we were quiet out of respect for the other people who were praying in church. Until one morning . . .

We were going in to daily Mass. Liz was at my side, skipping and singing at the top of her lungs, when I realized all the windows of the church were open. The words slipped out before I even realized I had said them. "Quiet down, now, we're going in God's house."

She looked up at me, somewhat startled, but made no comment. As we entered the side door of the church, the door to the sacristy was open in front of us. From the far end of the room, our assistant caught sight of us and bellowed in what can only be described as a booming voice: "Good morning, Elizabeth."

Balancing on tip-toe, (a tough task for a child not yet three), she walked the length of the room slowly and quietly. As she reached Father Paul, she put a finger up to her lips and said softly, "Shhh! God's sleeping!"

*　　　*　　　*

I think I have decided that reverence is the ability to stand in awe before the mystery. If this is true, one look at a child chasing a butterfly, searching for the heart of a flower, or studying the reflection in a pond is enough to convince me that children are born reverent.

Lord, in my effort to help my children develop socially acceptable behavior, let me never tamper with what you have already taught.

Cal

"I hate God! I hate Him! I asked God to make Cal better and he didn't. I'm never going to pray to him again!"

My five-year-old stamped her feet as she screamed, tears streaming down her face, frustration, rage and grief overwhelming her. It was the ultimate nightmare that every parent fears; if we teach our children to pray, what happens when God says "No"? I held my little ball of fury in my arms and wondered what I had done wrong. Cal was a young father from our family religious education group. He had developed cancer six months earlier and we had all prayed for him to get well. There didn't seem to be any other reasonable way to pray. But what could I tell my child that could possibly make sense? I didn't understand. I was suddenly filled with rage at a God who could allow such injustices, who would let a young father die. I had taught my child to trust this God and God had proved unfaithful. I had done nothing wrong. It was God's problem and God could take care of it!

"Liz, you go sit on your bed and you tell God exactly how you feel. You let God know you are very angry and that you think this is all God's fault. And you can punch your pillow, too."

She headed off to her bedroom, stamping her feet and slamming the door, and I sat at the kitchen table to pray—for Cal, his family, and the precarious faith of my daughter. I had visited Cal earlier that week in the hospital. No longer able to speak, he had opened his bible and shown me the passage about God concealing truths from the wise and revealing them to the simple. On a piece of paper he explained that God was teaching him to be a child again but it was hard, so very hard. I retrieved the crumpled paper from my purse and read his words again through my tears.

When my husband returned from work, I shared the news and asked him if he would talk to Liz. I no longer knew what to say. He returned in a moment, looking a little puzzled, and explained that Liz was singing and that she had a message for me. Reluctantly, I went to her room and perched on the end of her bed, taking note of her dry eyes and quiet smile.

"Did you talk to God?"

"Yes. And God talked to me."

"What did God say?"

"God said that Cal was very happy now.

"That's wonderful, Honey. What did you say?"

"I said, 'I don't believe you, God!'"

It wasn't what I had anticipated, but
say I was surprised. She had been very ang

"Mommy, God said that you would know. He
said to tell you that Cal loves being a child again."
She paused, looking at me with a slightly puzzled
expression. "Are you a child again when you go to
heaven? Is Cal a child again?"

I sat in stunned silence on the end of her bed.
There was no way my child could have known
about my conversation with Cal. The peacefulness
in her face told me that I did not have to assure
her it really had been God. The message had been
to assure me.

*   *   *

*Help me, Lord, to trust you with the faith of
my children.*

Rose

Rose was twenty-eight years old and she was dying. The lung cancer diagnosed only a few months before had metastasized to her heart. I sat next to the hospital bed and tried to pray with her, but she wanted no part of it.

"I hate God. I cannot look forward to going to a God who does not love me."

A God who loved her would have given her a child. She did not have to say it; I had heard it many times already. She and Bob were good people; they had prayed for a baby. They had tried to adopt and there were no babies. A God who would not bless their love with a child was not someone with whom she wanted to spend eternity.

Reasoning didn't help. It wasn't God's fault; it was the cancer already in her body, it was the people who chose abortion rather than have an unwanted child, who were the reason there was no baby. Frustrated by my own inability to get through to her, I wrapped my arms around this frail body and told her we would pray for a baby.

In the weeks that followed, I stopped at the hospital on the way home from school as often as possible, each time walking through guards with a pass that was boldly stamped "NO VISITORS," and each time praying with my dying friend for a baby. It all seemed crazy, the blindness of the guards, the unreasonable request, but I knew that Rose was not ready to go home to a God who had hurt her so badly.

She died on a Friday that I didn't make it to the hospital. Ed met me with the news as I walked in the door. Even though I knew she was dying, I couldn't believe she had actually gone, not before that prayer was answered.

The doorbell rang. Her husband came into the kitchen from next door and held me in his arms while we both cried.

"I have to show you something, Kathy." He pulled a legal looking document from his pocket.

"This came yesterday. It is from the Children's Center in Hamden. You heard about the Vietnam baby lift, didn't you?"

I had heard. The news was full of all the orphaned Vietnamese babies they were flying into this country. The whole operation had been dubbed the "baby lift."

"The Children's Center got several of these children. They have a baby for us; they needed to know if we still wanted to adopt. I took the papers into Rose last night and she signed them. Then she died in her sleep."

*   *   *

Lord, no matter how deep the darkness that follows, it is impossible to deny that blinding flash of light. What does it take for us to believe? Water from the rock? Three little fishies? Or a baby for a dying friend?

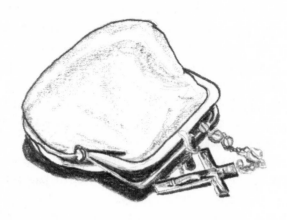

A Little Hope

I was alone in the old stone Gothic structure, my sobs creating a hollow echo in the dim coldness. Nothing in life was going right, not even this visit. I had come seventy-five miles to this parish to talk with a priest friend about the mess I was in, and he had been called away to the hospital.

Kneeling in a pew half-way down the aisle, I yelled at the empty stone interior: "I'm not asking you to change anything, God. All I want is the courage to go on. All I need is a little hope. Is that too much to ask, just a little hope?"

The door opened in the rear of the church and I covered my tear-streaked face, praying that the person entering had not heard the last shouted phrase. The sound of heavy footsteps making their way up the aisle, followed by light, quick ones, signaled the presence of an adult and a small child.

From the front of the church, I heard a woman's voice explaining the creche that was still up from Christmas. Then the steps started down the aisle. The heavier ones passed me, but the small ones stopped near my elbow. A voice whispered, "Don't bother the lady. She's praying."

I was not praying and I have a great deal of respect for little children, so I looked up to find out what this little one wanted. My gaze met the most beautiful pale blue eyes I have ever seen. They were in the face of a very small child, no more than three, who was standing a yard or two away. We looked at each other intently for a moment, then she trotted directly over to me and placed a hand on my arm.

"I'm Hope," she said clearly.

Not "hello," not "my name is," just "I'm Hope."

Startled, I took her arm and snapped at the mother, "Is that her name?"

Frightened by the wild look on my face, she grabbed her child, answered, "Of course!" and ran from the church.

That's not what I meant, God! But I had to admit, she was even a "little" Hope.

*   *   *

If humor is part of what makes us human, and if humanity is created in the image and likeness of God, then, God, you must have a wonderful sense of humor. If I had not believed it before, Hope has convinced me.

Crutches

"Religion is just a crutch. So is God."

It seems to have become a fashionable thought among the teens, just the old "opiate-of-the-masses" idea, clothed in new words.

How did "crutch" ever acquire such a pejorative connotation? The implication is that being "crutch" somehow makes God and religion less real. Anyone who can say that has never used crutches for very long.

I rely on a cane. It enables me to do things I could never do without it. My little electric cart is another crutch. With it, I am practically indefatigable on shopping expeditions or sight-seeing jaunts that my own legs could never handle.

A crutch does not change reality; it helps us to deal with it more effectively. Glasses are a crutch. They do not change what is in our view, they correct our vision so that we can see it more clearly. Hearing aids are a crutch that allow us to hear what is actually going on when our own ears muddle and muffle the sounds.

Is religion a crutch? Is God a crutch? Probably. I certainly know it enables me to deal with life in those areas where I am most limited, to see better those things I am most likely to distort, to recognize cries I might otherwise ignore.

*　　　*　　　*

If we cannot accept the crutch of religion or God, I suspect it is because we have not yet come to terms with our own limitedness.

College Returnees

My son is home from his junior year at college. You could not prove it by his presence at the supper table, by long, cozy parental discussions, or even by the possibility of a better distribution of chores. I suspect I see less of him than when we made a point of driving to the campus visiting. But there are signs, nonetheless.

The phone rings incessantly, and the message board is covered with calls for Jon. The washing machine runs mysteriously in the middle of the night, along with the vacuum cleaner, if there is a hold on the car until chores are done. Music occasionally blares up from his room, indicating, not only his presence, but some strenuous form of exercise that will leave the downstairs fragrant. The size of the phone bill clearly indicates that, while he may not always talk to us, he is talking to

someone.   He continually dashes through the
house, to work, to a friend's, to a race, leaving behind a wake of lights, towels, and empty juice bot-
tles. He has no time.

I suspect, many of us have the same kind of relationship with God. We need God to be there for us,
providing and sustaining. We will turn to him/her if
the troubles get big enough and we can't handle
them alone any more. We may even have a conversation, if there is no one else around. But have a real
relationship with this God? We have no time.

*   *   *

God, are you waiting for us all to grow up?

Deck Prayer

The 7 a.m. school bus is gone and I have the house to myself. This is my favorite time of the day, before the breakfast dishes are cleared, before the computer is turned on, before the work of the day is begun. I fix my second cup of tea and retire to the deck that perches like a tree house behind the second level of our home.

The leaves have eaten up the sky above me. Only glimpses of blue are visible through the heavy canopy of green created by the hickory and maple that crowd the house. God seems distant, like the sky, blocked from view by the busyness, the confusion of incidentals in my life. Miscellaneous thoughts litter my prayer as the leaves clutter the sky.

In the midst of my inability to pray, my frustration threatens to give way to sadness. From somewhere deep inside me an awareness forces itself to the surface. There is, after all, no sky out there; it is a mirage. It is no more, no less, than the air that surrounds me, that fills my being with each breath.

I breathe deeply, take a sip of tea, and am content.

*　　*　　*

"Close behind and close in front, you fence me round, shielding me with your hand."
—Psalm 139:5

Plants

The plants in the house are in desperate need of a little attention. Most of the time, we make sure they get some sun, some water, and a little fertilizer, and they do just fine. But it is time to prune and re-pot, wash the dust off the leaves, and generally spruce them up.

When we first built this house, I asked all our friends to make cuttings of their plants and start them for us. I knew this was going to be a great house for plants, with all its skylights and glass, and I wanted something living to remind me of the important people in our lives.

Today, as I dig and prune, I am aware of how much like the friends who gave them these plants are. Most of the time, it does not take a great deal of time and attention to keep friendship alive, but it does take a little consistency. Eventually, though, there needs to be some quality time together to become re-rooted in all the things that first brought the friendship to life.

*　　　*　　　*

Neglect is deadly for all living things.

The Rock and the Sand

Standing on the edge of the rock, I watched the waves of the Atlantic come crashing in, spraying me as they hurled themselves against the line of boulders that marked this stretch of the Gloucester shore. The ocean has always been my image of God: its power, its constancy, the steadiness with which it is always coming, the life teeming in its depths. And I am like the rock, resistant, unchanging, confronting the approaching water with an unyielding wall, sending the waves shattering in all directions.

I walked away, saddened by the knowledge of my own recalcitrance, and sought some solace on the quieter shore of the bay. Here, the sand gave easily beneath my feet, and the waves crept in gently, washing away the footprints in my wake.

I want to be like the sand, Lord, gently moved by each touch of the water, receiving, changing, accepting the presence of the sea.

As I stood on the shore praying, the answer to the prayer was suddenly audible in the wind and the surf.

"My foolish Child! Do you know what you ask?
The sand is nothing but the rock—BROKEN."

* * *

*The dangerous thing about praying is not that
You do not listen, God, but that we so often get exactly what we pray for.*

Part III

Belonging

Belonging

There are only two lasting bequests we can give our children; one is roots, the other is wings.

—Anonymous

Nothing connects us radically to the earth like the birth of a child. There is a realization of all the outside influences that will come to bear on the life of this child, the larger community, the town, the church, the generations that have gone before and those that will come after. This awareness creates in us, as parents, a desperate need to be part of the community that will touch and influence this child, to be able to assist in shaping the world that will insist on shaping the child.

One of the first lessons our children teach us is our need for a church. If the Church were to do away with the custom of infant baptism (as it has considered), I suspect parents would invent their own sacrament. A child reminds us that we need a community that roots us in a common past and provides hope for a common future. Its traditions form part of our understanding of who we are, its rituals guide us through transitional and difficult moments, its stories offer insight into our own stories.

We decided when our children were quite young that they were never going to understand what it meant to be church on the parish level unless we also provided a more immediate and personal understanding of community. The family community that grew out of that decision shaped our own idea of church and strengthened our bonds as family, while it provided the vehicle for handing on our religious tradition. Our children were as much teachers as learners, offering their own insights to taken-for-granted truths, their own applications for stories we had allowed to sit trapped in books.

We called our community FIRE and many of the following stories flow from that community's understanding of belonging. They are stories about growing up Catholic, but they can easily be understood in the light of any strong, religious tradition.

Creation

The decision not to send our children to traditional religious education programs, but to teach them in a family community, was not arrived at without a great deal of personal uncertainty and doubt. Like most parents who choose alternative methods, I was paranoid about whether or not my son, our eldest child, was "getting it." Had anyone asked me what "it" was, I doubt I could have explained. But whatever "it" was, I was not convinced my son was "getting it."

To settle my own anxiety, I gave my second grader the Confirmation test designed for the parish eighth graders. This was not quite as farfetched as it sounds. He could read on an eighth grade level, and I wasn't expecting him to get *all* the answers, just enough to reassure his mother.

Jon breezed through the test easily, stumbling over a question on "conscience" (a new word) and missing completely a question on creation. The true/false statement read "God revealed himself fully in creation." The eighth graders were expected to choose "false" and then list the principal means of revelation which they had memorized.

Some of them even did that! Jon had circled "true."

"Jon," I countered, more than a little disturbed. "You know that isn't true. You know that God is revealed in the prophets, in Jesus, in . . ."

"Mommy," he interrupted, "It doesn't say that God is revealed *only* in creation. It says 'God revealed himself fully.' I think he did. Then he had to send all those other things because we didn't hear what God said the first time."

*　　*　　*

They call it original sin. Bernard Haring, noted moral theologian, defined it as the failure to respond to the fullness of God's plan in creation. My son, at seven, called it the failure to hear what God said the first time.

Lord, I think he's getting it.

Swimming

The pool at the YWCA was closed today. All the three-year-olds met in a classroom to learn strokes and breathing techniques. It was hilarious to watch, and had the kids not been enjoying themselves, it would have been totally pointless. It is simply not possible to teach swimming outside a pool.

*   *   *

I wonder, Lord, if it is any different from trying to teach children about God in a classroom?

Parable

One of the new people in our FIRE group was deeply disturbed by our study of creation. She had never before noticed that the two stories in the first two chapters of Genesis were completely different.

"But which one is true?" she asked with agonizing uncertainty.

Before I could answer her, Jon chimed in. "They are both true, they are just not true the way history is true or science is true. They are true the way a parable is true."

*   *   *

Teach us, Lord, to listen to the understanding hearts of our children.

Convention at the Jordan

We were building our own house and had run out of time and money simultaneously. We had to sell our home in order to continue building, but it left us with no place to live. Friends lovingly offered us the basement of their home, a fairly small area with two rooms and a bath. We spread mats on the floor for sleeping, rolling them in the morning to make room for fixing breakfast. We used the window sills for refrigeration (it was a very cold winter) and tried to make do.

Our three children, thirteen, twelve and eight at this time, managed our homelessness with the resilience that only belongs to the young. Ed and I grew more and more depressed and tense, as he dragged himself home from his regular job each day to work with me on a house we were beginning to hate. We were barely speaking to each other or the children.

One night at supper, through silence and tension as thick as pea soup, eight-year-old Liz brightly announced, "This is just like the sojourn in the desert."

We looked at her glumly. "What are you talking about?"

"Remember the lesson about the Israelites in the desert when Moses died?"

We had done a lesson in our FIRE group the previous winter about the attempt to choose a new leader after the death of Moses. By studying the Book of Numbers, we had identified four dissenting groups among the Israelites. There were those who always wanted to turn back at the first sign of trouble, the ones who constantly moaned, "Oh for the leeks and garlics of Egypt." We called them the Whiners. The tribes of Rueben, Gad and the half tribe of Manasseh, who had wanted to stay in the desert because it was good for raising cattle, were called the Nomads. The Spies had been the strategists who went out with Joshua and were constantly studying ways to take the land; and the Priests were the tribe of Levi according to whom it would all work out if you only said the right prayers and followed the correct rituals. While I remembered the lesson, I had no idea what it had to do with our living in the basement of a friend.

"What are you talking about, Liz?"

"Don't you see? This is our sojourn in the desert. We are trying to get to our own promised land and we have all the different groups right here in our family. Becky and me are the Nomads; we could live here forever."

She and Becky liked living in this house in the middle of town, where they could walk to school, and the library, and the pharmacy.

Becky caught on and joined the story. "Jon is the whiner. Every time something goes wrong he says 'Why did we ever have to leave Oxford?'" She imitated his voice, throwing in the whining quality the group had perfected at the FIRE meeting. "Dad's the Spy. He is always looking for new ways to get money for one more thing, or a little more time to do something else."

"And Mom's the priest," the three ended in unison. "Just say the right prayers and it will all work out."

We laughed together for the first time in a long time. For the rest of the five months that we shared that little apartment, any time anyone would complain, someone else would say quickly, "Oh, for the leeks and garlics of Egypt." It saved our marriage, our family, and our sanity.

*   *   *

The real power in Scripture, or in any story, is in allowing it to become our story.

Being Catholic

Liz had a special invitation for Good Friday. Passover was falling on the same day this year and her best friend in third grade had invited her to the family celebration. While we had held a couple of Seders in the parish, this was the real thing.

Liz came home bubbling with enthusiasm and insight.

"I know the difference between being Catholic and Jewish," she declared emphatically.

"What is the difference?" her dad asked curiously.

"When you are Catholic, everything important happens in Church. When you are Jewish, everything important happens at home."

*   *   *

That is a terrible indictment on us, my child, and shows a serious Catholic misunderstanding of sacrament. Everything important happens at home for us, too. We simply go to church to ritualize and celebrate it.

Mudpuddles

The parking lot was clear and dry; only one corner contained a residue of water from the storm. Every child leaving church who was not firmly held by the hand found that one puddle. Several good Sunday outfits were promptly splattered with muddy water while little plastic dress shoes were subjected to abuse they were never meant to handle. The delighted squeals of the children mingled with the terse orders the adults shouted after them.

How many times have I told a child "Watch out for the puddles!" How many pairs of shoes have I stuffed with newspaper when my warnings were forgotten or ignored? While my children outgrew the shoes, the habit lingered on. In high school it was running shoes that fell victim to deliberately muddy cross-country courses, and soccer cleats that showed the effects of puddles.

What is it that is so inviting about water? How wise the church was when it chose water as its symbol of welcoming!

*   *   *

"All you who are thirsty, come to the water."
—Isaiah 55:1

Lent

I grew up firmly convinced that Lent had some intrinsic connection to candy; you did without it completely for six weeks, then you got enough on Easter morning to make you sick.

It was a Friday in Lent, a vacation day, and I was picking up Liz and her two friends from the skating rink. They were starved and we decided to stop at McDonald's. As we pulled into the parking lot, I remembered the day and turned to apologize to my daughter.

"It's Friday. You can't have meat."

Her Jewish friend, Nora, long familiar with the traditions of kosher, was instantly interested.

"Can you have the fries or are you not allowed to have anything cooked in animal fat? They will cook them specially for you, if you ask."

Liz looked at me questioningly, and I explained that the restriction was simply on eating meat.

Kristin, the third girl in the back seat, said, rather wistfully, "We don't have anything special like that in our church."

I am not sure if doing without meat, and having a shake and fries instead, fulfills any sacrificial function, but I was aware of it doing something far more important that day. It gave my daughter a sense of belonging, a sense of who she was as a Catholic.

*   *   *

You don't need our sacrifices or our rituals, God. We do. We need them to know who we are, to know who you are, to know who we are in your presence.

The Reign of God (1)

We sat around the fire enjoying the unexpected luxury of a "snow day." Taking advantage of the family being all together in one spot at one time, I pulled out the family religious education homework. (There are times when it is tough to be the children or spouse of a religious educator!) The story we were sharing compared the reign of God to a Coke bottle washed up on a desert island shore.

"That's dumb." My fifteen-year-old was objecting. I had chosen the story for the group and actually thought it was pretty clever.

"Do you think you could do better, Jon?"

"Sure. We all could. You can compare the reign of God to almost anything."

It was too good a challenge to pass up. The story given here is the record of the family dialogue that followed.

The Reign of God (2)

It was a blustery, cold day. The snow was falling in sheets as the family sat companionably
around the fire. A bowl of popcorn was being
passed among them and the buttery smell mingled
with the aroma of the soup simmering on the stove
when a knock on the door disturbed the quiet.

A tall stranger stood before them, laughing
and shaking the snow from his beard. Could they
offer him temporary shelter from the storm? In
moments, his wet coat and gloves were hanging by
the fire, room was made in the circle for him, and
a steaming mug of soup was placed in his hands.
The family was too polite to question what had
brought him out in such weather, and they waited
in comfortable silence for him to speak. His first
words shocked them.

"The reign of God is like a blizzard."

All eyes turned questioningly toward him.

"Yesterday, the raindrops were transparent
and plain. You could look right through them.
but today, the cold has turned them into crystals,
each magnificent in shape and design, each unique
and beautiful. The reign of God is like that.

"Yesterday, the world was drab and gray. But today it is made new! The snow fell without a sound, transforming the earth overnight; only the wind announced its coming. The reign of God is like that.

"Old modes of transportation won't work; we must find new ways of getting around. Yet, we resist changing and attack with plows and sand and salt. So it is with the reign of God.

"The reign of God is like the blizzard. It draws families together, slows people down, isolates them from all that could distract them from each other. It makes us dependent on one another for help—and shelter."

Here, he smiled gently at the family that had taken him in.

"The reign of God is like that," they responded.

The eldest child, a boy of fifteen, looked thoughtfully at the bowl of popcorn in his lap. He spoke quietly.

"The reign of God is like popcorn. It comes to you in seed form and it looks rather hard and unappetizing. It takes warmth to make it burst forth into food. The reign of God is like that.

"There is something about popcorn that is just made for sharing. It makes so much more than you expect that there is always enough to go around. The reign of God is like that."

The stranger nodded appreciatively as the youngest child spoke up.

"The reign of God is like vegetable soup. It warms you all the way through. It's very nourishing, but only if you eat it. And what makes it taste so good are all the different kinds of things that are in it. The reign of God is like that."

She concluded by climbing into the stranger's lap and snuggling her head to his chest. He smoothed her hair back gently and his eyes came to rest on the middle child. The most reticent of the three, she read the invitation in his look and spoke quietly.

"The reign of God is like the fire. It brings light into the darkness. You can stand far away and only see the light. You can move closer and you will feel the warmth. But if you were to jump into the fire, you would be totally consumed and transformed. The reign of God is like that."

The family sat quietly, each one wrapped in thought. In the silence, they realized the wind had died down and the snowfall had turned to a gentle flurry. Each one dreaded seeing the stranger leave.

Sensing their thought, he said softly, "I am always with you; no farther away than your love for each other."

They helped him with his coat and boots and gloves. He paused at the door just long enough to smile and say:

"The reign of God is among you."

Body of Christ

Our FIRE meeting was focusing on the second reading from Sunday's liturgy, the Corinthians passage about being members of one body. People were grouped by families, discussing together what parts of the body each of them represented.

When we reassembled, everyone shared. Some of the responses were predictable; a lot of Mom's were seen as the heart, a lot of Dad's as the hands. Some were funny, like the Dad who was beginning to feel like the butt because everyone had been sitting on him lately. Liz, as the only child left at home, had dominated our discussion,

"In our family, Jon is the kidneys. He is critical and points out bad things all the time, but that is okay because it brings them out in the open and you can flush them out of the system.

"Becky is the skin. She is the one who connects us all to each other, but she is also the most fragile, the most sensitive, and we all tend to take care of her.

"Mom is the spinal cord. She is sort of the message center for the family, sending out the information to each part, in touch with each of us all the time.

"Dad is the backbone. He is the strength of our family, what holds us up, and he is the protective casing around the spinal cord.

"I'm the voice. I say the things everyone thinks but no one says out loud."

*   *   *

You are also the eyes, Liz. You challenge us with the vision of childhood and the intuition of the young adult, both competing in your person to be heard.

Confirmation

Shotgun weddings are considered invalid, not sacraments at all. Yet shotgun confirmations seem to be the norm.

Chip was a student in the eighth grade confirmation class in a parish where I served as DRE. He came regularly every Monday evening, and just as regularly, got thrown out of class. One Monday, I sat with him and asked: "Chip, why do you come here?"

"'Cause I gotta."

"Why do you gotta, Chip?"

"Cause I gotta get confirmed."

"Why do you have to get confirmed, Chip?"

The answer was simple and immediate. "So I don't have to come here any more."

Years later, Liz and our auxiliary bishop collided at the coffee urn at the same parish's silver anniversary celebration. He smiled warmly, introduced himself, and asked if he had confirmed her yet. I tried to intervene to divert the conversation, but I was a second too late.

"No, Bishop. I am not going to get confirmed."

"Why?" he asked gently.

"I'm not sure I believe everything that the Catholic Church teaches and Confirmation is saying I agree."

"Do you study about the faith?"

"Oh, yeah, I've been in a family religious ed program since before I was born. I just still have a lot of questions."

"Well, being confirmed does not necessarily mean you are certain of everything. It means you are as sure as you can be and you believe that the Roman Catholic Church is basically the right choice for you, even if there are still things that trouble you."

It was a reasonable explanation and I had used it many times myself. This had become a familiar conversation in our house; I knew what Liz would respond.

"But, Bishop, I would be saying I want to be Catholic for the rest of my life. I don't know what I want to be tomorrow, let alone for the rest of my life."

"Do you pray about it, Liz?" I was relieved and grateful he didn't say "child." At fourteen, it is an insulting familiarity.

"You mean, do I pray about whether or not I should get confirmed? No. I don't exactly pray about things. I pray—it's just not like that. It's more like wanting God to be with me or being grateful or just sharing something happy, like you would with a friend. I don't ask God if I should get confirmed. I don't think God cares."

"Well," the bishop responded, "I hope you will choose to get confirmed because the church needs you. If I do get to confirm you, please remind me that you are the person that shared jelly dough-nuts with me. I may forget your face, but I won't forget our conversation."

* * *

It is possible to present religious education as a lifelong process with confirmation an option along the way. The problem with giving options in any-thing is that we need to be ready to live with the choices that are made. At what point do we stop saying we know what is best for you? Is it our tim-ing that is so wrong? Is it really unjust to ask you to make a "forever" commitment when you are not sure what you want to do with your life tomorrow? Does God care?

"The will of God for you is this: that you rejoice always."
—1 Thessalonians 5:18

Jesus and the Eucharist

Most of all, I remember his eyes. They were that pale, pale blue, that sparkles and reflects the color of the sky. They seemed to look right through you, but with such kindness that no one could ever be afraid.

His name was Father Hughes. He had announced at Mass that the final practice for First Communion would be at the summer religion school on Monday morning and the children would celebrate on Saturday. At six years of age, I was too young, not only for that class, but for any of the summer classes. As we walked out of church, I looked into those eyes and, to my parents' utter amazement, asked if I could make my First Communion.

My parents tell me that he asked me several questions and was delighted with how well my mother had taught us all our catechism. I only remember his eyes looking kindly at me and my mother's increasing nervousness. She was nine months pregnant with my little sister. She might not even be around on Saturday and there could be no new dress and no party. I turned and reassured her that I didn't care; I only wanted Jesus.

I looked back up at those eyes in time to see them fill with tears. I remember very little about the liturgy and the day, but I will never forget the look in those eyes, and the love and respect they held for me and for my decision. Much of my present image of God is tied up with that look.

Years later, my own son, at six, confronted a pastor with the same question. This time, I was the mother who was surprised. This time there was none of the gentle acceptance I remembered from my own childhood. The priest assumed a rather combative tone and asked, "You probably don't even know what I do up there at the altar, do you?"

Incensed and wounded, Jon responded in the same contentious manner. "If you are going to try and tell me you change the bread and wine into Jesus, you're wrong, 'cause I listened to you. You ask God the Father to send the Holy Spirit down on the gifts so that they can become the body and blood of Jesus."

Rattled by the bold response, the pastor turned away abruptly with some dismissing remark about precocious children. This time, it was the child whose eyes filled with tears.

*   *   *

If we invite our children to belong, we must be prepared for them to have their own ideas about church, their own timetable for sacraments. There may be reasons, although I would question them, for insisting a child wait to receive Eucharist. There is never a reason for ignoring the spiritual life of a child or for treating his understanding or desire with contempt.

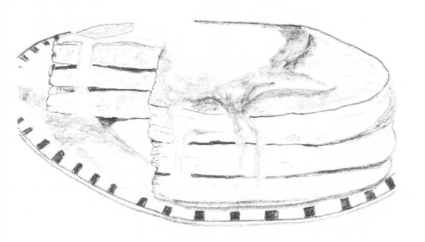

Pancakes

My mother made the best pancakes in the whole world. At least, growing up, I always believed she did. Pancakes were a ritual in our house. We would wake to the smell of pancakes and hot syrup and come running down to find my Mom at the stove. She would pile a plate high, place it in front of my older sister who left for school first, and say, "Your mother makes the best pancakes in the whole world."

Next, she would fix plates for my younger brother and sister, set them on the table in front of them and say, "Your mother makes the best pancakes in the whole world."

I usually got to the table last and would receive my plate of pancakes with the same ritual comment, "Your mother makes the best pancakes in the whole world."

Last of all, my Mom would sit down with her own breakfast. As she placed her plate on the table, we would all chime in, "Our mother makes the best pancakes in the whole world," and I firmly believed she did.

All my growing up years, no one could place a plate of pancakes in front of me without eliciting the comment, "My mother makes the best pancakes in the whole world." It did little to endear me to the mothers of my friends.

As I grew older, though, I started to taste other people's pancakes. Some of them were quite good. Some of them were even better than my mother's!

I was not at all certain what to do with this knowledge. My mother and I had always had a very open relationship and I needed to tell her the truth. One Saturday morning after I had turned twenty-five, I was home and Mom was making pancakes. As she placed each plate on the table she said, "Your mother makes the best pancakes in the whole world." It was now or never.

"Mom," I started off gently, "I've been tasting other people's pancakes."

She smiled and said, "I'll bet some of them are quite good."

I was relieved to know that she knew.

"Yes."

"I'll bet some of them are as good as mine."

As she said this, she put another plate of pancakes on the table, saying, "Your mother makes the best pancakes in the whole world."

"Some of them are probably even better than mine."

80

She smiled and put another plate of pancakes on the table with the same ritual comment.

"Mom, if you knew that," I asked, "why have you been telling me all my life 'You're mother makes the best pancakes in the whole world?'"

"Kathy, what do you think of every time you see pancakes?"

"I think, 'My mother makes the best pancakes in the whole world.'"

"And what do you think of every time you eat pancakes?"

"I think of you."

My mother smiled and nodded.

"As long as there are pancakes, you'll remember me."

*   *   *

And Jesus said, "Whenever you eat this bread or drink this cup, do it to remember me."

Part IV

Journeying

Journeying

Life is so full of meaning and purpose, so
full of beauty—beneath its covering—that
you will find that earth but cloaks your
heaven . . . we are pilgrims together, wend-
ing through this unknown country home.
—Fra Giovanni (1513)

A poster hung in the family room of our old
home. It read: "Life is a journey, not a destina-
tion." Traveling the road with children is a con-
stant reminder of the truth of that poster, a con-
stant invitation to see the heaven cloaked in the
milestones of earth.

These are the stories about growing, the simple things that every family confronts along the
way. They have become moments of revelation
and insight for us, moments to understand a little
more fully the journey we share. In many cases,
they are lessons our children have taught us, lessons I suspect, we might not have learned without
them.

Boys and Dolls

Jon wanted a doll for Christmas. He was not yet three, his mother had a new baby, and all the stores were advertising "Rub-a-Dub dolly." It seemed like a reasonable request and we made sure Santa honored it. His paternal grandfather who had raised three boys (most certainly without dolls) had a fit!

Later, when Becky was nine and wanted a Huffy boy's bike so that she could go tearing through the woods and around the neighborhood, no one objected. Her Christmas request that year for a racetrack didn't even raise an eyebrow. She was considered "one of the boys" by her male peers and her tomboy ways delighted the older male members of the family.

Why is maleness the norm, acceptable in boys and girls, and femininity the aberration? Why is it that women who dress in a masculine way get jobs as executives and men whose clothes even hint at feminine get excluded and ridiculed?

*　　*　　*

And why is it that we have all heard a thousand sermons on the good shepherd (we even have a Good Shepherd Sunday) and no one mentions the woman and the lost coin, the matching parable in which God is a woman?

Training Wheels

We were standing in the aisle at Toys 'R Us. We had decided to buy Jon a two-wheeler for his birthday, but he seemed far from happy about the decision. He had not yet mastered the art of riding and, as I studied the troubled expression on his face, I began to realize that what I was seeing was fear. He moped among the bikes and I began to have second thoughts. Perhaps this was not a good idea; perhaps we should wait for a moment less strenuous and demanding than a birthday.

I pulled Ed aside and started to explain my concerns quietly when Jon came charging down the aisle on a little red bike.

"Look, Mommy, Daddy! This one has little wheels!"

*   *   *

How did we neglect to tell you, son, that they all come with training wheels?

Life itself comes with training wheels. Let us be there for you, ready to offer balance and support while you learn to ride; hopefully willing to be set aside when you are able to ride on your own.

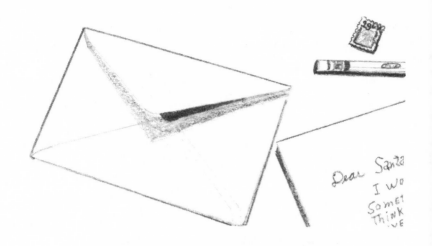

Santa and Other Truths

"I never got to go see Santa."

It was Christmas Eve, complete with more than the usual chaos, as we planned for the on-slaught of the entire family. The bread still needed to be baked, the custard sauce prepared for the plum pudding, a few last minute gifts wrapped, and the kitchen floor dug out from under a two week layer of flour and sugar. Nine-year-old Becky stood stubbornly before me.

I am not a hard-hearted mother, but you have to understand. In nine years, this child had never been willing to see Santa Claus. Each year, we faithfully brought her, and, other than the very first year, when we took a picture of her screaming on his lap, she had refused to go near the man! She would always want to go, right up until the moment she saw him. This year, I had decided we could do without the yearly tearful ritual; I wasn't even sure she believed any more! So I had taken her little sister alone.

"Becky, today is such a busy day and the plaza will be mobbed. I really didn't want to have to leave the house. Couldn't we write him a letter and leave it with the cookies? I'm sure he knows what you want."

At this point, it really would have been easier to simply point out the truth, whatever that was, but I have never been totally convinced myself that there is no Santa Claus.

I looked at my nine-year-old. Tears were beginning to fill her eyes.

"Are you sure? You always say you want to go and then change your mind once we get there. I just don't have time for that today."

"I know, Mom, but this time I'm sure."

There was something in her voice that persuaded me. For reasons I could not understand, this was terribly important. We would have to go.

Fifteen minutes later, after a terrible ride in the sleet and the snow, I was not so sure. There was not a parking place to be had in the whole lot, and so I asked once again, "Are you sure, Becky?"

"Yes, I'm sure."

After forty-five minutes searching, I was growing frantic. We drove by the little store that had been decorated as Santa's workshop.

"Could I let you off and come and pick you up? There really is no parking." (This was, after all, the child who handled the dentist and orthodontist confidently on her own.)

"Please come with me, Mom." I tried to ignore the whine creeping into the voice, tried to tell myself that years from now she would have happy memories of this moment.

The parking spot we found was on the other side of the plaza.

"Before we walk all the way over in the sleet, Becky, I want to know that you really want to do this. Are you sure?"

"Yes."

We arrived at Santa's workshop desperately needing some hot chocolate in the empty souvenir cup the elves handed us. We were soaked to the skin, but Santa's line had been mercifully shortened by the weather. As we headed toward the queue, Becky grabbed my hand.

"Please don't be angry, Mom," the tears were starting as she spoke, "I don't want to go."

At that moment I understood how people manage to dislocate children's arms. We have all been tuned into the problem of child abuse. What about parent abuse? What about all the work that was waiting for me at home? What about the floors and the bread and the presents, and the simple fact that I was now soaked and exhausted?

I bit my tongue, took her hand gently, and walked out of the store. I was far too angry to risk speaking. She cried all the way across the parking lot. But in the car, she settled down contentedly, too contentedly, as far as I was concerned. We began our silent drive home.

"I think that's stupid." Her voice startled me.

"What's stupid?" I asked between clenched teeth.

"Dressing somebody up in a red suit and having people come and tell him what they want for Christmas. It's dumb."

I must admit that my first reaction was to throw my child out of the car! I resisted the impulse and sat quietly thinking through what had just happened to us.

Some myths die hard. It is a scary thing to let go, even when a part of us can no longer accept what is obviously not true. There is always the fear that we will never be able to find the real truth hidden in the myth. It is definitely too scary a thing to do alone.

*   *   *

Give me patience and love for the growing, Lord; it comes at such inconvenient moments. Thank you for a child who makes the pain visible and insists that we be there with healing and hope.

Braces

Becky needed braces. It is hard to convince a three-year-old that if you suck your thumb it just may come back to haunt you. It was even more difficult for a nine-year-old to believe that something that looks so ugly and makes you feel so conspicuous was worth the effort.

She started with a bionator and only graduated to wires when her jaw had grown. At every appointment, the wires were tightened ever so slightly, then the teeth would be given another six weeks to adjust to their new position. The idea was to make no more demand on the teeth than they were ready to accept and remember.

*   *   *

Help me, Lord, to be as patient and consistent with the emerging person as the orthodontist is with her teeth.

Retainers

Teeth have a memory. Once you have taken the braces off, if you left the teeth alone completely, they would go back to their original position. The trick is to release the tension slowly by wearing a retainer. The retainer gently holds the teeth in place and is worn less and less as the teeth gradually remember on their own.

* * *

Retainers are for the adolescence of teeth.

Becky's Party

Becky wanted a sleepover for her ninth birthday. I hate sleepover parties. One friend overnight, or even two, is fine; sleepover parties tend to be all night disasters with crabby children, made miserable by their lack of sleep, fighting over breakfast in the morning. I gave in, on condition there were only four guests (a house rule with some precedents), pointing out that this might make for a small, rather quiet party, and might also limit the games that could be played.

Becky was thrilled anyway. She had four close friends and it would have all worked out fine, but one of her friends had a twin sister. The parents did not allow either girl to go anywhere unless both were invited. I was thoroughly annoyed; Becky did not even like the sister, but the twin was her best friend. I offered to call the parents, rather than bend my own rule, but Becky chose to be generous and invite the twins as two of her four guests.

On the day of the party, long after the first two girls had arrived, we waited for the twins. As the pizza started to get cold, I asked Becky to call and make sure they weren't lost. A few seconds into the conversation, her face started to change; she barely managed to get off the phone before bursting into tears. The twins' mother had told her that one of the girls had done something wrong and they were both being punished. They weren't coming to the party.

As I held my crying child in my arms, I wondered if this mother knew that the person she had punished most was my daughter. She had dominated her invitations and then demolished her party without even the courtesy of a phone call. Becky had done nothing wrong except to try to comply with an adult's unreasonable rules. The lesson was clear: adults are not necessarily fair and the grown-up world is not to be trusted, at least not until it proves itself worthy of that trust.

The prophet Jeremiah said that each person is to suffer for his/her own sins. (Jer 31:30) This mother taught us the importance of never discipling in a manner that punished another child for our own child's behavior. We held to that rule all through the growing up years. I never met this mother, and it took me a long time to forgive her, but I am grateful for what she taught us.

*   *   *

Those who hurt us frequently teach us far more than those who never offend us. Help us, Lord, to let go of the pain long enough to be able to grasp the lesson.

The Closet

I sat calmly on the edge of the bed as my eleven-year-old daughter violently emptied her closet. In her own mind, she had come of age, and she could no longer wear all those "nerdy" things her mother had lovingly chosen for her. In middle school, you are what you wear and no one would want to risk looking like her mother.

My serenity in the face of such obvious rejection had less to do with spiritual detachment than with the fact that this was the third child of the family. I already knew how this scene was going to end. Quietly, I folded and sorted clothes for relatives and charities, while my daughter heaped abuses on my taste in everything from sweaters to raincoats. The bed was quickly covered and the closet bare. I waited.

"Well," she said, eyeing a loved sweater on the top of the charity pile, "I think I might keep this one. I picked it out, didn't I?"

With great fortitude, I kept a straight face. A smile, a laugh, any hint of an "I told you so" would be deadly at this point. I bit my tongue and offered a hanger,

"I guess I'd better keep the skirt that goes with it." Another piece returned to the closet.

Gradually, the pile on the bed went down and the closet began to fill. Yet the contents were different, now. They were not the clothes her sister had loved and outgrown, the clothes her parents had bought for school or her relatives had given as gifts; they were the ones she had chosen.

*   *   *

An important part of growing up is discovering for ourselves what are our values, ideas and beliefs. Let the pre-adolescent closets in our house remind us, Lord, that only those things we are free to reject are we ever truly free to call our own.

On Materialism

Twelve-year-old Becky was bemoaning the limited size of her budget allowance for new school clothes.

"I wish we had millions of dollars so we didn't have to worry about it and we could buy all the clothes we wanted."

"Even if we did have millions of dollars," I responded, "With so many people in the world having nothing, I would find it hard to spend that kind of money on clothes."

"Well, I wish we could all be equal and everybody have the same," she countered quickly.

"That's a noble thought, Becky, but do you realize if that were true, the only clothes you would own are the ones you have on?"

She paused a moment, looked down at herself, and responded, "Could I change first?"

*   *   *

Materialism dies hard!

Guardian Angel

Liz got in with the wrong seventh-grade crowd. It is the thing every parent dreads, but no one prepares us to deal with it. The group clung to each other, devoured each other, and radiated distrust and trouble from the lunch table where they congregated. The other students wisely avoided them. We watched Liz's frustration and unhappiness grow deeper and deeper until we finally handed her an ultimatum. "Change lunch tables or change schools."

It sounds simple to those of us who have forgotten what it feels like to be twelve and to desperately need to be part of a group, any group. If she left the only group that welcomed her, would there be others willing to be her friends? The trouble with that question was that she would never know the answer without first taking the risk.

I have doubted, for a long time, the church's teaching on guardian angels, but an angel came to her aid that day. The lunch tables were only a few yards apart, but Liz still describes changing tables as the longest walk she ever took. The aide who was supervising situated herself firmly between the two tables, making eye contact between the groups seated at them almost impossible. For the next few weeks, Liz avoided the lavatories when "the group" was in them, and worked at staying out of lonely corridors. Through it all, the protective presence of the aide lingered near her.

Fortunately for Liz and for us, others who had avoided her reached out quickly and became her friends. A few from the original group followed her lead and tried to leave the table. Some made it. In every case, the same protective shadow covered them.

I may still have questions about the existence of angels, but I know for a fact that Liz has a guardian angel. I have seen her. I even know her name.

*　　*　　*

"He will put his angels in charge of you to guard you; they will hold you up on their hands in case you hurt your foot on a stone."

—Ps 91:11-12

Decisions

The hardest decisions to make are the ones between two goods. The choices between good and bad are easy. Even the choices between two bad things: always choose the lesser of two evils. But when we are faced with two good choices, the family outing or the friend's birthday, piano lessons or soccer, those choices are sometimes heart-rending.

Liz made the All-State chorus, one of her high school's first two sopranos and the first PHS sophomore to do so. At the same time, she got a much-desired role in a community theater production of *Oliver*, and both were rehearsing and performing at the same time. Rejecting All-State meant that she would be barred from participation the following year. Despite pressure from school, tearful tirades, and a few sleepless nights, she followed her heart and did *Oliver*.

I kept waiting for the regrets to set in. Each time she would come home from a tough rehearsal, I would expect to hear "I should have done All-State." It never came, and in the weeks leading up to both performances, my daughter taught me a whole new meaning to "Blessed are the single-hearted, for they shall see God."

*   *   *

"If only" is definitely one of the more serious sins in my life. Regrets frequently clutter my enjoyment and cloud my perspective of any chosen good. While Liz learned a great deal from her community theater experience, I expect I learned more. The lesson of Oliver is clear: make a choice then live with it wholeheartedly, soaking up the pleasure and bearing with the pain that comes with any choice. Those who put their hand to the plow and look back are not fit for the reign of God.

College Applications

Becky keeps putting off filling out those horrendous college applications. Last year, when we argued about this with her brother, it was not as surprising. Natural procrastinator that he is, we knew he would wind up paying overnight mail charges on most of them. But Becky does everything weeks in advance, everything until now.

The problem is not the applications, it is the fear of being rejected. This is more important than trying out for the team or the history day contest. This is the rest of her life, at least in her eyes. And the fear of being rejected is not half as bad as the fear of being accepted and the decisions that will entail.

*   *   *

Becky, few decisions in this life are engraved in stone, or even written in ink. Most of the lines we make are in pencil, and they can be erased. What is possible, what seems best for today, is the only choice any of us are capable of making. God's presence is rarely in front of us, clearly showing the way. More often, God dwells inside us, guiding

and enabling the choices we make, and "All things work together for good in those who love the Lord."
—Romans 8:28

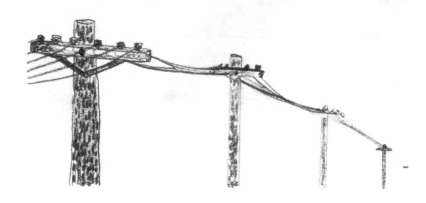

Tears on the Telephone

There is nothing in the world as frustrating as tears on the telephone. As I listen to your anguish, I want you back under my roof, safe in my arms, where, if I can't fix the problem, I can at least soothe the hurt. But you are on your own, miles away in your college dorm, with only a wire connecting us. No matter how hard I try, I cannot reach through the plastic, the transistors and the cables to touch your pain.

*   *   *

God, you are not limited by distance and telephones. Wrap your arms around my almost grown child and offer the comfort I can't seem to give.

Silverware and Other Changes

Becky came home for Christmas from her freshman year at college. She was different, older, somehow, more independent, but it did not take long before we realized that she was not the only one who had changed. It became obvious when she opened the silverware drawer. We had switched the teaspoons with the forks, and moved the tablespoons over from another drawer. She was appalled.

She complained for several minutes about the total insanity of the new setup, while I listened with my mouth open, completely stunned by her reaction. The silverware (a misnomer for our K-Mart cutlery) simply did not deserve this kind of attention. As she presented her case for putting things back the way they were, the truth dawned.

"Becky, this is not about silverware. You are angry because you went away and things didn't stay the same while you were gone."

I tried to talk quietly about all the things that had changed: the babies who had grown older since she baby-sat for them, the tree in the yard that had died, the schedule for chores that made allowances for one less person helping out. Life still went on even when she wasn't there. I tried to be reassuring; she had changed but she still loved us, we would change while she was gone but we would always be her family. I hugged her and figuratively patted myself on the back. I thought I handled that crisis fairly well.

As she turned to leave the room, her parting comment was, "I still think its a lousy place to put the forks!"

*   *   *

Help us to remember, Lord, that we are not the only ones experiencing the trauma of letting go.

A Real Devil

"Well, what do you say, do you think it was a real devil?"

We all turned bewildered eyes to my son, home from college the first weekend in Lent. We had no idea what had inspired the comment.

"Where, Jon, in the meat loaf? Do you want to tell the rest of us what we are talking about?"

"In the desert, in that reading from the gospel last Sunday. There is an older woman [this usually means thirty-five] in our discussion group at school who thinks it was a real devil. What do you think?"

If there is anything I have learned from my teenagers it is that "What do you think?" is not a question. It is simply a linguistic device that means "Let me tell you what I think." I have discovered it is far simpler to just skip over what I think and ask "What do you think?" since this is what they are waiting to say.

"What do you think, Jon?"

"I think it was Jesus' coming of age, just like, for example, going away to college. There are certain temptations when you are trying to figure out who you are. He was tempted by all the same things. The first is the temptation to use your gifts for material gain. That was the bread. The second is to use your gifts for fame. That was the pinnacle of the temple. And the third is to use your gifts to get control over others. That was the cities of the world. I don't think there needed to be a 'real' devil. I think that the devil who tempted Jesus is the same one that lives in all of us."

*   *   *

Amen.

Neighbors

Our neighbors across the street have moved away. For four years we have lived opposite a white cape with a yard that looked like a picture out of *Better Homes and Gardens*. The banks on their driveway were lined with flat rocks that fit together like a giant jigsaw puzzle while they hugged the earth. Our drive is lined with grass trying to survive countless teen drivers, along with a few crocus that have escaped the former. Their flower gardens bloomed profusely each spring while those of mine that were not strangled by poison ivy were trampled by over-enthusiastic basketball and volley ball games.

The manicured lawn across the street stretches for three acres down what would be the best hill in the neighborhood for sledding, if anyone had been allowed to sled there. The snow in that yard stayed picture perfect, while ours was quickly trampled, dirtied and dotted with snowmen and forts. On occasion, our neighbor would venture over with his plow and clear our short, flat driveway. A welcome assist: we tend to treat snow the way we treat leaves. The Lord giveth and the Lord can take away.

On those rare days when their garage doors would be left open, it was easy to see our neighbor's neat array of tools lining the walls. Our garage (frequently left open) resembles a graveyard for things with wheels—bicycles, tricycles, strollers, skates and old lawn mowers. It even housed a broken down car before the vehicle made its way to a more permanent resting place.

Our new neighbors are younger and far less exacting. The grass is sprouting between the perfect rocks along the driveway, and the driveway itself is bearing the marks of neighborhood skateboards as the children discover it is now safe territory. The flower gardens are a little unkempt this year, occasionally raided by the preschooler who stays with her grandmother two houses down. The lawn is trimmed far less frequently, and I suspect it will bear sled marks in the wake of the first snowfall. They remind me, this childless, thirty-something couple, that there are more important things in life than exterior perfection.

I still look forward to a day when grass and crocuses will be allowed to grow around our house and the garage will actually house the car, but I can wait. There is a lot to be said for having a basketball hoop in your driveway, a volleyball net on your lawn, and a snowman in your yard.

Part V

Becoming

Becoming

Parentage is a very important profession;
but no test for fitness for it is
ever imposed in the interest of children.
—George Bernard Shaw

We learn to become parents through parenting. We model some of the things that were done to us, or pattern our behavior on the opposite approach, but it is the everyday events with which our children fill our lives that eventually teach us how to parent. Unfortunately, by the time we become comfortable in our profession, the kids are usually gone.

The whole task is complicated by the fact that every child needs different parents; what worked so well with the first, fails miserably with the second, and has been forgotten before the third reaches that stage. And since we cannot help but grow and change ourselves, every child grows up in a different family.

These stories represent the struggle to become parents. After we have looked through the eyes of wonder with our children, fostered a prayer life, rooted them in community, and journeyed through the milestones, it is time to look at the vision we have gained through parenting. I am convinced that whether or not we are "good parents" does not depend on how our children turn out. We are good parents if we have become beautiful through the process of parenting. Ultimately, how our children turn out will be their own choice.

Stranger in My Home

Someone should have told me love doesn't come naturally. You can carry a baby in your womb for nine months and still find she is a stranger in your home. Perhaps it was because I nearly died giving birth. Perhaps it was because I only viewed her through a window while she hung suspended between life and death, a tiny china doll in a glass case, untouchable and remote. Perhaps it was because the blood loss and hormone imbalance created a horrendous postpartum depression that tore at the very core of my being.

Whatever the reason, the warm and cuddly feelings I had anticipated enveloping me as soon as I brought this baby home failed to come. It did not help that she cried constantly, fighting off with tiny fists every effort to hold and comfort. I cried with her, overwhelmed with frustration, bewilderment, and not a little admiration for this diminutive human being, so intent on surviving.

Ed and I took turns sleeping, longing for the day when she would sleep more than fifteen minutes at a stretch. Although he was every bit as tired as I was, her Dad was obviously enchanted by this startlingly beautiful little girl child. Why couldn't I feel the way he did? What was the matter with me?

I am not sure when she stopped crying, but it was about the time she started climbing. Soon there wasn't a surface in the house that was safe; we took her from the top of the refrigerator, the drapery rods, the chandelier. There wasn't a crib, car seat or harness capable of containing her. She wouldn't stay still long enough for me to love her, or perhaps I was just too tired to feel anything, anything but guilt.

A friend shared with me a practice of an early North American tribe. They believed that every child was a stranger in the house, someone entrusted to your care, whom you prepared for life and let go. It was a strangely comforting thought. It made no demands on my feelings; it only asked that I treat this child with the same gentleness and care that I would give to any child in my home, that I simply do the loving thing. Love, after all, is an action, not feeling.

Freed from the necessity of "feeling," I began to enjoy this bundle of energy who danced before she walked and made leaping bounds off any surface into the nearest available pair of arms. When she refused to sit still long enough for a story, I sang her a song. I stood over her crib in those moments she slept peacefully, wondering what long forgotten ancestor had endowed her with her beauty, and prayed for that rush of maternal feeling that always seemed just beyond my grasp.

We were sitting in the living room one night after her bath, rocking and singing lullabies. At three, my little stranger (as I often thought of her) was content to be quiet and cuddled and the touch of her soft skin mingled with the scent of soap and baby shampoo.

"Good night, my someone, good night, my love." The song from *Music Man* had long been her favorite, but that night the old words held a new sting. She looked up at me sharply, a hint of pain in her large, dark eyes.

"Mommy, I am not someone. I'm your Rebecca. Sing 'Good night, Rebecca, good night, my love."

I began the song again. "Good night, Rebecca, good night, my love." Suddenly, all the feelings that had eluded me for three years overpowered me, and I choked back tears as I sang. Even today, I cannot remember that moment without being overwhelmed with a love so poignant it still brings tears to my eyes.

*   *   *

Rebecca, "I have called you by name and you are mine."

—Isaiah 43:1

Good Babies, Bad Babies?

Jonathan was such a quiet baby. He would sit in the infant seat intently studying his hands, or rattle, or the rug. I could take him anywhere and people would always say, "He's such a good baby. You must be a wonderful mother."

Becky was hyperactive. If I took her anywhere at all, she would climb the bookshelves, knock over the lamps, and destroy anything within range (and everything was within Becky's range). Did this make her a "bad" baby? Was I now a terrible mother?

Babies are not good or bad; they are amoral. I might never have known that without you, Becky. Thank you for teaching me that I am not responsible for the personalities each of you have brought into the world, only for loving you and helping you to become all you hope to be.

*　　　*　　　*

Protect us, Lord, from the harsh judgements we place on ourselves for the personalities of our children.

Gifts of Love

We had all gotten up late. As fate would have it, it was library day and neither child could locate the books. Once that crisis was handled, Jon could not find his shoe. He was in special orthopedic shoes and since we could never afford more than one pair, it had to be found. By the time we discovered the missing culprit and I had him out the door, Becky had thrown herself down on the driveway screaming that she did not want to go to school. After the crazy hour we had just endured, I did not have the time or the patience for school phobia this morning. I walked down the driveway half pushing, half pulling, my reluctant kindergartner. The school authorities had insisted we shouldn't give in; she had to get on that bus.

As it pulled away, I tried to tell myself that all of this would soon pass. (In reality, Becky got over the school phobia very quickly, but Jon still can't find his shoes.) It wasn't until I turned back up the driveway that I realized I had left the youngest alone in the house. I dashed up to the back door, only to be greeted by an overpowering fragrance.

In the living room, my toddler stood in the middle of a literal snowstorm. She had just emptied my very expensive French Talc, an annual Christmas present from my husband, all over the rug. She had pulled out the vacuum cleaner, although she had no idea how to use it.

"I help. Make Mommy feel better," she lisped, a self-satisfied smile spreading across her face.

I suppose my talcum, that I stretched so sparingly through every year, resembled the powdered cleaner I used on the rug, at least to an almost two year old person. I know she was offering the best antidote she had to a difficult morning, a little helping hand. The tears were a mixture of frustration and love, as I wrapped her, the empty cannister, and the vacuum in my arms.

*   *   *

Teach me, Lord, to look beyond the unacceptable gift to the love that prompts the giver.

Lost

Dusk was just beginning to creep into the country kitchen at my parents' home. We glanced out the window occasionally while we cleaned up the supper dishes, keeping a careful eye on our three-year-old son as he chased his grandparents' dog around a grassy yard nestled at the edge of the woods. Suddenly, he was gone. Ed and I ran outside calling, expecting to hear him answer at any moment. We were not overly disturbed; it had only been seconds since we had last seen him. But the seconds turned into minutes and the irritation to apprehension.

Ten minutes later, we called the police. The neighbors my mother had called were beginning to arrive when the fire department and police vehicles pulled up. In seconds, the fire chief had organized the searchers into a long line, each only a few feet from one another, as they moved forward into the woods. A camera crew from the local news station set themselves up in the driveway and I listened in a daze as a commentator talked to a camera about a three-year-old boy in an orange jersey and jeans who was presumed lost in the woods on Bishop Hill.

I began checking out the woods across the street where no one else had gone. Would Jon cross the street? He knew he wasn't supposed to go alone, but then, he wasn't supposed to leave the yard, either. Suddenly, I was furious and mentally promised myself he would stay in his room for a month once he was found. If he was found. As the minutes stretched into an hour, my anger turned to fear and I began to bargain with God. I would be such a good mother, I would never yell again, if only God would save my son.

I returned to the yard to find the chief calling in the searchers. It was growing dark and they would not be able to do any more until morning. He held up a little muddy shoe as the camera man moved closer. (Some disassociated part of my brain registered that this would be a moving shot.) Was it Jon's? (Oh yes. We had paid forty-five dollars the day before for those orthopedic shoes!) It had been found at the edge of the swamp bordering the lake far behind my parent's home. There had been footprints in the mud going into the water, but none coming out. The fire chief explained gently that they would drag the lake in the morning.

Before the significance of his words sank in, there was a shout from the edge of the woods. Ed was running toward me with our son in his arms. Anyone who does not understand the father in the story of the Prodigal Son, the father who asked no explanation, no promises of reform, no acts of sorrow, has never known what it is to lose a child.

When that child is found, there is no room for anything but joy.

*   *   *

"We are going to have a feast, a celebration, because this son of mine was dead and has come back to life; he was lost and is found."
—Luke 15:24

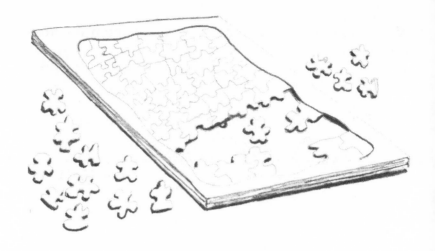

Try, Try Again

Two-year-old Liz banged the wooden puzzle piece with her fist, furiously trying to fit it into the wrong space. I wrapped my arms around her angry little body, extracting the offending piece from her fingers.

"Where do you see this color?" I prompted. "What part of the body do you think this might be?"

She took the piece, put it back in the same spot and went back to hammering angrily.

This time, I took the piece away, placed a different one in her hand and angled it carefully. It slipped easily into the stubborn spot, and she applauded delightedly.

*   *   *

I am not sure that "If at first you don't succeed, try, try again" is a good maxim for children, or adults, for that matter. Some pieces simply don't fit in certain spots, no matter how long or how hard you try. And some pieces may fit, but not the way you anticipated.

So, if at first you don't succeed, try differently. If that fails, try something else.

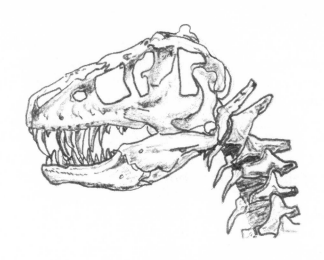

"Holy Family"

I grew up with a deep devotion to Mary. However, the whole idea of her being the perfect mother was wearing thin by the time I had children of my own. After all, I could probably have been a perfect mother, too, if I had Jesus for a son.

We had taken the children to the Peabody Museum in downtown New Haven to see the dinosaur exhibit. At five, Jonathan was already reading well and had become an expert on dinosaurs. We lingered as long as we could before the massive skeletons, then toured the rest of the museum. Liz had fallen asleep in the stroller and four-year-old Becky was starting to tire when we realized Jon had disappeared.

An hour later, after the museum guards had been alerted and the building thoroughly combed, our anger and frustration had given way to panic.

Downtown New Haven was not the place to lose a five-year-old boy, even a bright, self-sufficient one. We returned to the dinosaur room one more time; it seemed the only logical place.

In the far corner, a tour group stood listening in the same spot they had occupied on our last frantic trip through the room. We decided to interrupt and ask if anyone had noticed a tyke of five with curly brown hair and a striped tee shirt. Approaching the group, we heard a small, familiar voice explaining why the skeleton in front of them was included in the exhibit of this particular prehistoric age. The adults were listening with respect, crowding closely around this littlest paleontologist. All the fear I had been trying to quell came to the surface in one tremendous rush of rage. But before I could say a word, a voice somewhere in the back of my mind whispered softly "Son, why have you done this to us? Behold, your father and I have sought you sorrowing."

*   *   *

Perhaps raising a gifted child, being a "blessed mother" was not all it was cracked up to be.

Bubbles

My mother taught me, as a small toddler leaning over the sink, to blow bubbles on the surface of the water. First, we rubbed our hands with soap until they were slick. Then, making a circle with our forefingers and thumbs, we dipped the fingers into the water and blew gently on the film that clung to the circlet. The bubbles sat lightly on the surface, our breath encased in the fragile membrane.

I have taught my children to blow bubbles in the sink. I have watched, entranced, as they played with "bubble stuff" in the back yard, blowing bubbles through plastic wands, each tiny breath captured in a transparent film that turned sunlight into rainbows. Just as God once breathed life, so my children repeat the wonder. Who is to say which is the greater miracle?

*   *   *

Stars and atoms have no size,
They only vary in men's eyes.
. . . There is, in God's swift reckoning,
A universe in everything."
                    —A. M. Sullivan, *Measurement*

The Tooth Fairy

Where did we ever get the tooth fairy? Easter bunnies and eggs, Christmas trees and Santa, all have roots in ancient or Christian traditions. (My college son discovered that the Easter bunny comes from a pagan name for the first moon of the spring equinox.) But where did we get tooth fairies?

When Jon was six, he lost his first tooth. I had no idea that losing a tooth could be traumatic. Perhaps it has something to do with losing a part of ourselves. We cut nails before babies are old e-nough to be aware of the loss, but I wonder how many three-year-olds worry about haircuts. When people have limbs severed, we sometimes bury them respectfully, so why shouldn't we do some-thing with teeth?

I suspect the tooth fairy is needed to reassure us at a very vulnerable age that no part of us is ever truly lost. The reality of our self continues on, rewarded for surrendering a small portion to death. It is not enough, though, for this good fairy to leave us money; it is important, vital, that the tooth be collected, taken to live somewhere else.

Perhaps the tooth fairy, along with The Velveteen Rabbit and Cinderella, should be entered into childhood annals as symbols of resurrection.

*   *   *

"There is no need for you to be afraid. Why, every hair on your head has been counted."
—Luke 12:7

Lefty

"Are you all right?"

"No. I'm half left."

It's a dumb joke. But why should "right" mean "correct" or "okay"?

Becky is left-handed. For her, the glass is not on the right side of the plate; it's on the wrong side. So are the knife and the spoon.

After several weeks in first grade, Becky came home teary-eyed with a mutilated assignment in her hands. The paper involved was divided into two columns with geometric figures on the left side and empty boxes on the right. The student simply had to reproduce the figures in the empty boxes; Becky had failed miserably.

"I can't do it, Mommy, and everyone else can."

I sat down at the table with her and asked her to show me how she copied the first figure. As soon as she started, the problem was obvious. In order for her to write, her left hand was covering the figure she had to copy. I cut the paper in half and taped it so that the blank boxes were on the left of the figures and she finished the assignment easily.

*   *   *

Discrimination comes in a thousand ugly forms, limiting each of us, punishing us for being different. The "same" way may be the "right" way, but it is not the only correct way, and it may not work for everyone. We need to risk finding what works best for us. And it may not be the "right" way. It may be left.

Lefty, Revisited

Becky has a poster on her wall:

"If the right side of the brain controls the left side of the body and the left side of the brain controls the right side of the body, then only left-handed people are in their right minds."

Mirror Image

My daughter stood in front of the bathroom mirror and, like most teenagers, she was unhappy with what she saw reflected there.

"Why am I so ugly?"

I suddenly remembered another bathroom mirror and a similar comment out of my own past. My own mother, who had been passing by as I grumbled about my lack of beauty, had laid a hand on my shoulder and said:

"Don't you dare criticize my handiwork!"

I strongly suspect God is saying the same thing.

*   *   *

"Before I formed you in the womb, I knew you, before you came to birth, I consecrated you."

—Jeremiah 1:5

Helium Balloons

I have always loved helium balloons. Even now that my children are grown, it is fun to walk through an airport or mall with a balloon and watch all the babies faces turn up in pleasure, and listen to the toddlers who delightedly lisp "balloon." It defies all they have previously learned about the earth and gravity. It suggests things don't always go down when they fall. There are those few precious things, like kites and bubbles and balloons, that defy the rules and invite you to wonder.

When Becky was a toddler, she was like greased lightening. If I took her shopping, she would slip out of the stroller and, in the few seconds it would take to check behind the tall racks, she would be gone. Once, after telling her I did not have the money to fill her empty juice cup with soda, I found her, empty cup in hand, telling total strangers she needed money. They were delighting her by dropping coins in her cup! After that, I always bought a helium balloon on a long ribbon and attached it to her wrist as soon as we got into the mall. If she escaped the stroller, I could spot the balloon and reach her before she got into trouble.

This summer, we went to the airport to meet our foreign exchange student from Chile. As we got out of the car, our welcome balloon escaped across the parking lot. The "I love Connecticut" pin tied to the ribbon, however, kept it from drifting skyward, and Ed quickly retrieved it.   I couldn't help thinking what a wonderful image for our relationship with God. There was the urge to move upward that kept it suspended above the earth, the pin that grounded it in love for the earth , and the ribbon that connected the two.

*   *   *

Help me to understand and respect the ribbons in my life, Lord; family, friends, church, all the realities that connect me to you and ground me with the earth.

Warning Lights

The engine on the old Toyota seized up. It wasn't that Jon didn't see the oil light go on; he simply didn't believe it. There was so much wrong with the electrical system of the car that he felt reasonably sure this was just one more fluke. And the engine died.

*   *   *

My friend had a heart attack. It was not that he didn't have any chest pain to warn him; he simply didn't believe it.

*   *   *

Acquaintances of ours are getting divorced after twenty-two years of marriage. The warning signs have been there for a while; they chose not to look.

*   *   *

And when I was complaining about our Toyota to a friend, she told me that her teenager had pasted a smiley face over the warning light in their car because it had been annoying her!

*   *   *

A movie I once saw about an alien showed him learning to drive by watching humans. He explained what he had learned in this manner: "Red means stop. Green means go. Yellow means speed up and go as fast as you can." Collectively, we have convinced ourselves that warnings are not to be taken seriously. And so we jeopardize our posessions, our families, our very lives, by failing to believe them.

*   *   *

Slow me down, Lord, enough to take the warning lights in my life seriously.

Memories

My children's happiest memories are of the summers we spent camping. Neither Ed nor I are great outdoors people. We camped because it was affordable. In the beginning, we camped near all the wonderful educational sites we wanted them to see. But it did not take long for us to discover that what they remembered were not the historic places, scenic routes, and game farms; they remembered the "in-between" moments of camping.

We abandoned our attempts to create meaningful memories and returned each summer to the campground they loved. Today, they remember the tame skunk that visited us every night, the shooting stars we watched lying on the tail gate of the station wagon, the small nature center with the live snake and the parachute. The little beach on the lake where we rented the canoes, the beautiful rainbows after the thunder showers, the bike rides from east beach to west beach, are all treasured memories, stored carefully and shared lovingly at family celebrations.

My children eventually got to Disney World, Williamsburg and Busch Gardens. They don't talk about it much when we discuss family vacations. But they still laugh together about walking through the woods with a flashlight to get to the rest rooms, scaring the bats in the old tower, collecting firewood and carrying water.

I have often wondered what made camping so special to them. Perhaps it is that they were not expected to learn and appreciate, they could just play. Perhaps it is that the things that were expected of them, like keeping water supplied, were necessary and important, but well within their ability. Perhaps it was simply that their parents were not distracted by a hundred other things and had time to enjoy them.

The other day, I stood at the stove warming left-over macaroni in a pan. A broken microwave had forced me to resort to a method I had set aside with the dawn of electronics. My fifteen year old slipped her arms around me from behind.

"You know what is one of my happiest memories, Mom? We were in our old house and you were fixing left-over macaroni and cheese for me for lunch, just like this. You pulled a chair over to the stove and let me stand on it and stir, and you said you had to be careful not to add too much milk."

*　　　*　　　*

The most important childhood memories are not made of important places and events. They are made of people and space and woven through with love.

Refrigerator Door

What did people do before they had refrigerators? I am not as much concerned about what goes into them. In another age, we would live in the village and shop each day for our perishables. There would be a root cellar and we would probably be able to buy ice. It is the refrigerator door that I would miss.

At any moment in our family's life, you could describe us well from all that clings to the refrigerator door. (Next to the door itself, some of the most important things in our life have been the magnets we use with it.) This door once held kindergarten pictures and little tests with stars, soccer schedules, choir lists and newspaper honor rolls with important names boldly circled. The pictures and tests gave way to computer report cards about the same time the soccer schedules were supplanted by track schedules and baby-sitting reminders. Family religious education homework has been fighting for a spot for years. Newspaper reports of track conquests and school accomplishments have come and gone in their time, along with party invitations and letters. Now college schedules, theater auditions, Peace Corps information, diet and nutrition hints cover the surface. Comic strips and political cartoons have grown more sophisticated with the kids, but the same crazy magnets live on.

This is our third refrigerator. We tried a bulletin board, but it just didn't work as well. No matter where we put it, it was never as accessible as the fridge. I wish I had saved all the things we removed from that surface. Compiled in a scrap book, they would represent an accurate, all-encompassing family history.

If I had to list the truly important things in our home, the refrigerator door would be right up there with the dinner table: a spot for communication, recognition, and family reminders, a holding place for unresolved decisions. Refrigerators are a place of preservation, but the refrigerator door in our home has preserved far more on the outside than it ever did on the inside.

Waiting

The staccato sound of unison taps assaults my ears as I poise on the edge of a hard chair in the stuffy waiting room. At a pause in the clattering, the music from the group singing ensemble floats from another room, while the quieter sounds of my daughter's ballet class struggle for a spot in the cacophony.

How many hours, weeks, months have I sat waiting—in doctor's offices, dance studios, school hallways? How much of my life has been spent at soccer fields, spelling bees, concerts, and science fairs?

My life is marked into periods by waiting—the pregnant years, the well-baby visits, the braces years, the SAT and College response months. It has been riddled with moments of enforced quiet, invitations to contemplation. If Christians are the people who "wait in joyful hope" certainly parents have a lot to teach Christianity.

*　　　*　　　*

God, let every moment of waiting serve as a reminder to us to see the whole world through the eyes of expectant hope.

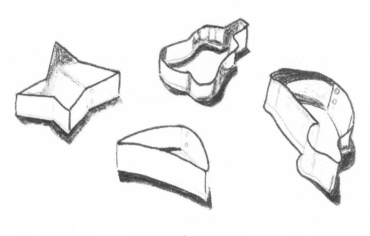

In Closing

There is nothing I can give you which you have not got; but there is much, very much, that while I cannot give it, you can take. No heaven can come to us unless our hearts find rest in today. Take heaven! No peace lies in the future which is not hidden in this present little instant. Take peace!

—Fra Giovanni

The words date back to a sixteenth century letter, but they are the words of every parent to every child. We have loved you, grown with you, changed because of you, but ultimately, it is all up to you.

*　　　*　　　*

I have a vision of all the parents gathered before God on judgement day. The Lord will say to us:

"I was hungry and you fed me, thirsty, and you gave me a drink, naked and you clothed me, homeless and you sheltered me, imprisoned and you visited me . . ."

And we will interrupt, protesting, "Not, I, Lord. When did I see you hungry and feed you?"
And the Lord will say:
"How could you ask, you of the three-and-a-half-million peanut butter and jelly sandwiches!"
"But thirsty, Lord?"
"I was in the kool-ade line that came in with the summer heat and the flies, and left fingerprints on your walls and mud on your floors, and you gave me a drink."
"But naked, Lord, homeless?"
"I was born to you naked and homeless and you sheltered me, first in wombs and then in arms. You clothed me with your love, and spent the next twenty years keeping me in jeans."
"But imprisoned, Lord? I know I didn't see you in prison. I've never even been in a prison."
"Oh, yes. For I was imprisoned in my littleness behind the bars of a crib and I cried out in the night, and you came. I was imprisoned inside a twelve-year-old body that was exploding with so many new emotions, I didn't know who I was any more, and you loved me into being myself. And I was imprisoned behind my teenage anger, my rebellion, and my stereo set, and you waited outside my locked door for me to let you in.
"Now, Beloved, enter into the joy which has been prepared for you for all eternity."

Amen